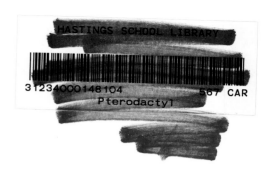
W9-CHP-619

Pterodactyl

Aaron Carr

MIGHTY DINOSAURS

www.av2books.com

Step 1
Go to **www.av2books.com**

Step 2
Enter this unique code

APVTH1Q2P

Step 3
Explore your interactive eBook!

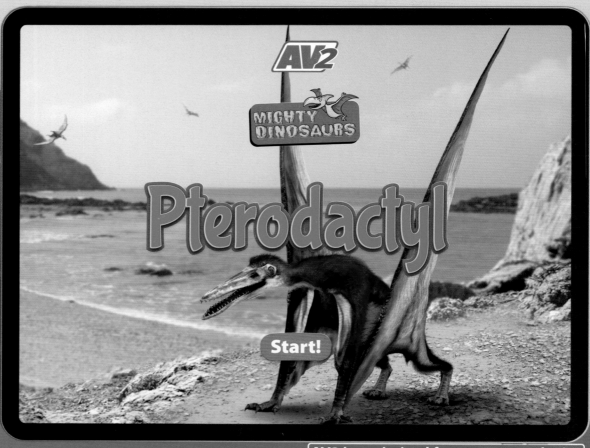

Your interactive eBook comes with...

Read

Audio
Listen to the entire book read aloud

Videos
Watch informative video clips

Weblinks
Gain additional information for research

Try This!
Complete activities and hands-on experiments

Key Words
Study vocabulary, and complete a matching word activity

Quizzes
Test your knowledge

Slideshows
View images and captions

View new titles and product videos at
www.av2books.com

?

Pterodactyl

CONTENTS

Meet the Pterodactyl.

Its name means "winged fingers."

6

Pterodactyl was a meat eater. It ate fish and other small animals.

Pterodactyl had a very long jaw with almost 100 sharp teeth.

13

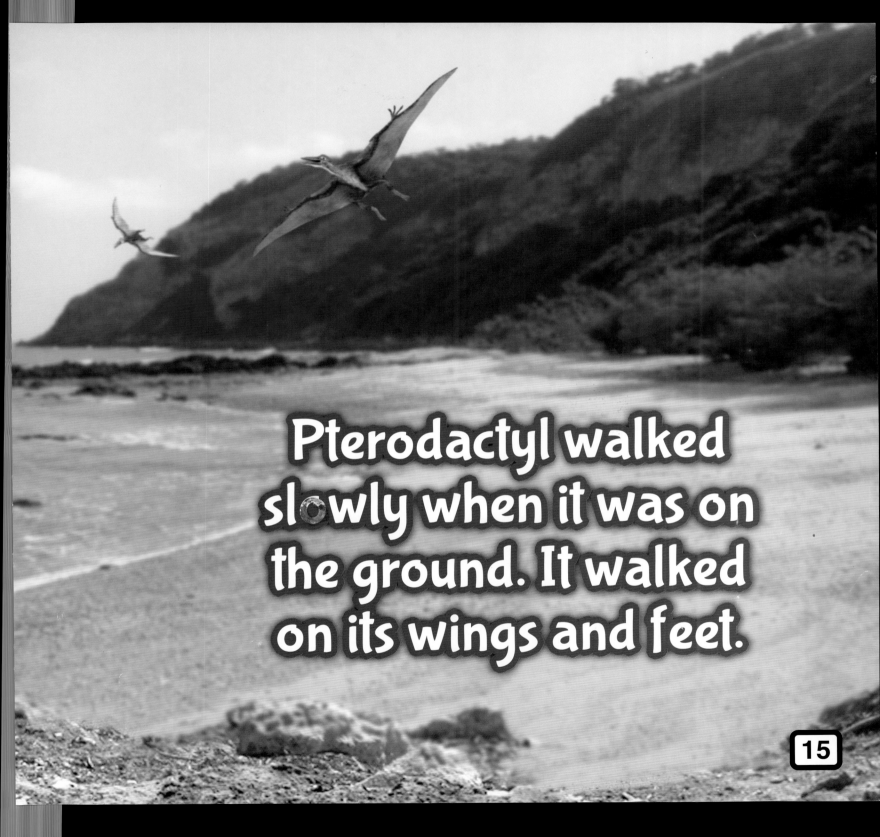

Pterodactyl walked slowly when it was on the ground. It walked on its wings and feet.

Pterodactyl lived in trees and caves near water. It could be found in parts of Europe and Africa.

Pterodactyl died out about 150 million years ago.

Pterodactyl fossils formed over millions of years.

People can go to museums to see fossils and learn more about the Pterodactyl.

The American Museum of Natural History in New York has Pterodactyl fossils on display.

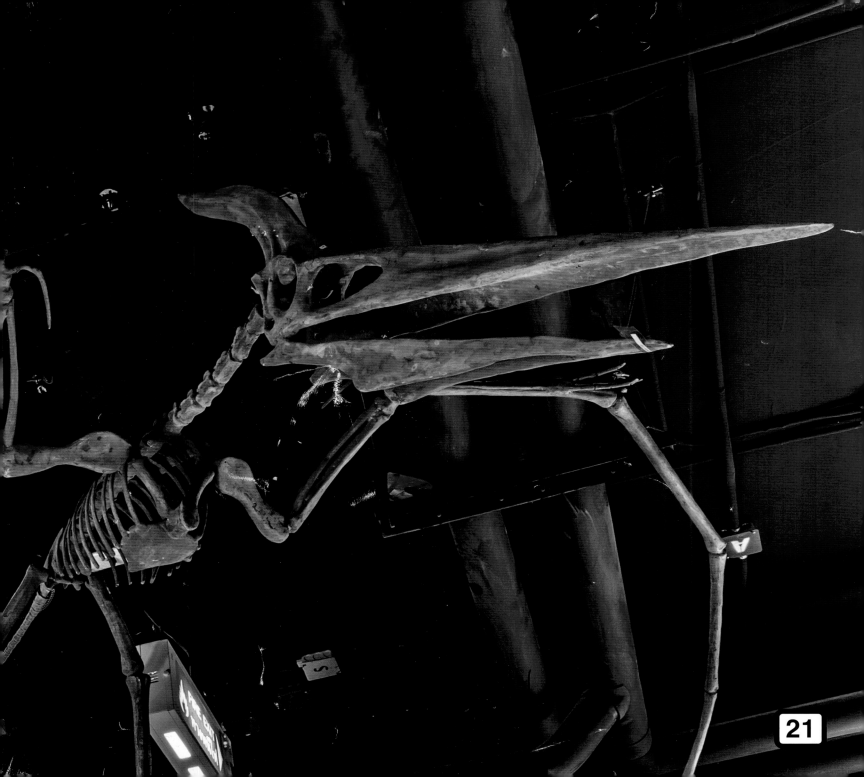

Pterodactyl Facts

These pages provide detailed information that expands on the interesting facts found in the book. They are intended to be used by adults as a learning support to help young readers round out their knowledge of each amazing dinosaur or pterosaur featured in the *Mighty Dinosaurs* series.

Pages 4–5

Pterodactyl means "winged finger." Though pterodactyl is a better-known name, this prehistoric animal's real name is Pterodactylus. The Pterodactylus was named for its long fourth fingers, which provided support for most of each wing. There were many different species of Pterodactylus. They ranged in size from as small as a sparrow to about the size of an albatross, one of the largest birds in the world today.

Pages 6–7

Pterodactylus was not a dinosaur. Dinosaurs were prehistoric reptiles that walked on land, while the Pterodactylus was a prehistoric reptile that could fly. For this reason, the Pterodactylus is not considered a dinosaur. Instead, it is part of a group of flying reptiles called pterosaurs. Pterosaurs lived in all parts of the world at the same time as the dinosaurs. Pterosaurs ranged in size from the small Pterodactylus to the massive Quetzalcoatlus, which stood as tall as a giraffe and had a 40-foot (12-meter) wingspan.

Pages 8–9

Pterodactylus had wings up to three feet (one meter) wide. The Pterodactylus had long, thin wings covered in skin. It had three fingers sticking out of the top middle part of the wing. The fourth finger on each wing extended about half the total length of the wing. The wing was formed by skin and muscle that stretched from the arm and long finger to the hind legs.

Pages 10–11

Pterodactylus was a carnivore, or meat eater. The Pterodactylus was a carnivore that primarily ate fish and small animals. It is believed the Pterodactylus flew over bodies of water and swooped down to catch fish swimming near the surface. Scientists believe the diet of Pterodactylus may have included crabs, mollusks, and insects.

Pterodactylus had a very long jaw with almost 100 sharp teeth. The Pterodactylus's narrow jaw made up about three-quarters of the total length of its skull. Unlike other pterosaurs, which had jaws that curved upward, the Pterodactylus had a straight jaw. When young, its teeth were wide and cone-shaped. As it grew older, its teeth became narrower and more numerous.

Pterodactylus walked slowly on its wings and feet. The Pterodactylus walked on all fours, using both its hind legs and its front claws. The rest of the wing folded and pointed up while the Pterodactylus walked. This is very similar to how modern-day bats walk. Scientists do not believe Pterodactylus was very fast when flying, but they think it was able to fly long distances.

Pterodactylus lived in Europe and Africa. The Pterodactylus is believed to have lived mostly in what is now Germany. Scientists believe the Pterodactylus lived in trees or caves near large bodies of water. They did this to stay close to their primary source of food. Living in caves and trees would have also offered some protection against predatory dinosaurs.

Pterodactylus lived about 150 million years ago during the Late Jurassic Period. All that people have learned about the Pterodactylus has come from studying fossils. Fossils form when an animal dies and is covered in sand, mud, or water. This keeps the hard parts of the body, such as bones, teeth, and claws, from decomposing. The body is pressed between layers of mud and sand. Over millions of years, the layers turn into stone, and the animal's bones and teeth turn into stone as well. This preserves the size and shape of the animal.

People can go to museums to see fossils and learn more about the Pterodactylus. Every year, people from all around the world visit museums to see Pterodactylus fossils. More than 20 Pterodactylus fossils have been found, and most of them are complete skeletons. These fossils are often part of permanent exhibits in large museums. Sometimes small museums for short exhibits. The American Mus New York has many pterosaur fossils

KEY WORDS

Research has shown that as much as 65 percent of all written material published in English is made up of 300 words. These 300 words cannot be taught using pictures or learned by sounding them out. They must be recognized by sight. This book contains 51 common sight words to help young readers improve their reading fluency and comprehension. This book also teaches young readers several important content words, such as proper nouns. These words are paired with pictures to aid in learning and improve understanding.

Page	Sight Words First Appearance
4	its, means, name, the
7	a, it, not, was
8	feet, had, its, long, of, one, out, that, three, to, up, used
11	and, animals, other, small
12	almost, long, very, with
15	on, walked, when
16	be, could, found, in, lived, near, parts, trees, water
18	about, years
19	over
20	American, can, go, has, learn, more, people, see

Page	Content Words First Appearance
4	fingers, Pterodactyl
7	dinosaur, pterosaur, reptile
8	wings
11	fish, meat eater
12	jaw, teeth
15	ground
16	Africa, caves, Europe
19	fossils
20	American Museum of Natural History, museums, New York

Published by AV2
350 5th Avenue, 59th Floor
New York, NY 10118
Website: www.av2books.com

Library of Congress Control Number: 2019950227

ISBN 978-1-7911-1660-6 (hardcover)
ISBN 978-1-7911-1661-3 (softcover)
ISBN 978-1-7911-1662-0 (multi-user eBook)

Printed in Guangzhou, China
1 2 3 4 5 6 7 8 9 0   24 23 22 21 20

022020
100919

Project Coordinator: Priyanka Das
Art Director: Terry Paulhus

Every reasonable effort has been made to trace ownership and to obtain permission to reprint copyright material. The publishers would be pleased to have any errors or omissions brought to their attention so that they may be corrected in subsequent printings.

All illustrations by Jon Hughes, pixel-shack.com. AV2 acknowledges Alamy, Getty, and Shutterstock as its primary image suppliers for this title.